Better Homes and Gardens.

Baking

Easy Everyday Recipe Library

BETTER HOMES AND GARDENS® BOOKS
Des Moines, Iowa

EASY EVERYDAY RECIPE LIBRARY
Better Homes and Gardens® Books, An imprint of Meredith® Books
Published for Creative World Enterprises LP, West Chester, Pennsylvania
www.creativeworldcooking.com

Baking
Project Editors: Spectrum Communication Services, Inc.
Project Designers: Seif Visual Communications
Copy Chief: Catherine Hamrick
Copy and Production Editor: Terri Fredrickson
Contributing Proofreaders: Kathy Eastman, Susan J. Kling
Electronic Production Coordinator: Paula Forest
Editorial and Design Assistants: Judy Bailey, Mary Lee Gavin, Karen Schirm
Test Kitchen Director: Lynn Blanchard
Production Director: Douglas M. Johnston
Production Managers: Pam Kvitne, Marjorie J. Schenkelberg

Meredith® Books
Editor in Chief: James D. Blume
Design Director: Matt Strelecki
Managing Editor: Gregory H. Kayko

Director, Sales & Marketing, Retail: Michael A. Peterson
Director, Sales & Marketing, Special Markets: Rita McMullen
Director, Sales & Marketing, Home & Garden Center Channel: Ray Wolf
Director, Operations: George A. Susral

Vice President, General Manager: Jamie L. Martin

Better Homes and Gardens® Magazine
Editor in Chief: Jean LemMon
Executive Food Editor: Nancy Byal

Meredith Publishing Group
President, Publishing Group: Christopher M. Little
Vice President, Consumer Marketing & Development: Hal Oringer

Meredith Corporation
Chairman and Chief Executive Officer: William T. Kerr

Chairman of the Executive Committee: E. T. Meredith III

Creative World Enterprises LP
Publisher: Richard J. Petrone
Design Consultants to Creative World Enterprises: Coastline Studios, Orlando, Florida

ISBN: 6-76171-00015-8 1-929930-15-1

All of us at Better Homes and Gardens® Books are dedicated to providing you with the information and ideas you need to create delicious foods. We welcome your comments and suggestions. Write to us at: Better Homes and Gardens Books, Cookbook Editorial Department, 1716 Locust St., Des Moines, Iowa 50309-3023.

Our seal assures you that every recipe in *Baking* has been tested in the Better Homes and Gardens® Test Kitchen. This means that each recipe is practical and reliable, and meets our high standards of taste appeal. We guarantee your satisfaction with this book for as long as you own it.

*Cover photo: Cinnamon Swirl Bread
(see recipe, page 24)*

Home baking comes from the heart. There's nothing that connects you with family and friends and brings back memories of days gone by better than the marvelous flavors and textures of homemade breads, cakes, or cookies right from your own oven.

In creating this book, we wanted to capture the rich, emotional experience of baking for you while presenting a tempting collection of recipes. Throughout this volume, you'll discover specialties for every occasion: from flaky biscuits and moist muffins and tea breads to tender cakes and showy yeast breads. So don't hesitate—select a recipe or two and delight your family and friends with a baked-from-scratch treat soon.

CONTENTS

Giant Blueberry Muffins

If you prefer a dozen smaller muffins, spoon the batter into twelve 2½-inch muffin cups and bake in a 375° oven about 20 minutes or till golden brown.

2 cups all-purpose flour
¾ cup granulated sugar
2½ teaspoons baking powder
½ teaspoon salt
2 beaten eggs
¾ cup milk
½ cup melted butter or cooking oil
1 tablespoon finely shredded orange peel
1 cup fresh or frozen blueberries, thawed
Coarse sugar (optional)

Grease six 1-cup muffin cups. Set aside. In a medium mixing bowl stir together the flour, ¾ cup sugar, baking powder, and salt. Make a well in the center of the flour mixture.

In another medium mixing bowl combine eggs, milk, butter or oil, and orange peel. Add all at once to flour mixture. Stir just till moistened (batter should be lumpy). Fold in blueberries.

Spoon the batter into the prepared muffin cups, filling each almost full. If desired, sprinkle the tops with coarse sugar.

Bake in a 350° oven about 35 minutes or till golden brown. Cool in muffin cups on a wire rack for 5 minutes. Remove muffins from muffin cups. Serve warm. Makes 6 large muffins.

Nutrition information per muffin: 425 calories, 7 g protein, 60 g carbohydrate, 18 g fat (10 g saturated), 114 mg cholesterol, 522 mg sodium.

Freezing Muffins

The freezer is the perfect place to save those fresh-baked muffins for another time. Wrap the muffins tightly in heavy foil or place them in freezer bags and freeze for up to 3 months. To reheat frozen muffins, wrap them in heavy foil and heat them in a 300° oven for 12 to 15 minutes for 1¾-inch muffins; 15 to 18 minutes for 2½-inch muffins; and 25 to 30 minutes for jumbo-size muffins, such as Giant Blueberry Muffins (above).

Pear, Ginger, and Walnut Muffins

Chunks of pears and walnuts make these muffins real winners. The unusual addition of grated gingerroot makes them extra special.

2   cups all-purpose flour
¾   cup sugar
2   teaspoons baking powder
½   teaspoon salt
¼   teaspoon ground cardamom or
    1 teaspoon ground cinnamon
2   beaten eggs
½   cup cooking oil
2   tablespoons milk
1   teaspoon grated gingerroot
2   medium pears, peeled, cored, and
    finely chopped (1½ cups)
¾   cup chopped walnuts
½   cup raisins

Grease eighteen 2½-inch muffin cups or line with paper bake cups. Set aside.

In a medium mixing bowl stir together flour, sugar, baking powder, salt, and cardamom or cinnamon. Make a well in the center of the flour mixture.

In another medium mixing bowl combine eggs, oil, milk, and gingerroot. Add all at once to flour mixture. Stir just till moistened (batter should be lumpy). Fold in pears, walnuts, and raisins.

Spoon the batter into the prepared muffin cups, filling each ⅔ full. Bake in a 350° oven for 20 to 25 minutes or till golden brown.

Cool in muffin cups on a wire rack for 5 minutes. Remove muffins from muffin cups. Serve warm. Makes 18 muffins.

Nutrition information per muffin: 197 calories, 3 g protein, 25 g carbohydrate, 10 g fat (1 g saturated), 24 mg cholesterol, 118 mg sodium.

Cranberry Apple Muffins

Here's a great way to use leftover holiday cranberry sauce. But, don't wait for the holidays to make these, they're good all year round.

½ cup whole cranberry sauce
½ teaspoon finely shredded orange peel
1½ cups all-purpose flour
½ cup sugar
1 teaspoon ground cinnamon
½ teaspoon baking soda
¼ teaspoon baking powder
¼ teaspoon salt
1 beaten egg
⅓ cup milk
⅓ cup cooking oil
1 cup shredded peeled apple

Grease twelve 2½-inch muffin cups or line with paper bake cups. Set aside.

In a small mixing bowl stir together cranberry sauce and orange peel. Set aside.

In a medium mixing bowl stir together flour, sugar, cinnamon, baking soda, baking powder, and salt. Make a well in the center of the flour mixture.

In another medium mixing bowl combine egg, milk, and oil. Add all at once to flour mixture. Stir just till moistened (batter should be lumpy). Fold in apple.

Spoon the batter into the prepared muffin cups, filling each ⅔ full. Make an indentation in the center of each with the back of a spoon. Spoon about 2 teaspoons of the cranberry mixture into each indentation.

Bake in a 375° oven for 18 to 20 minutes or till golden brown. Cool in muffin cups on a wire rack for 5 minutes. Remove muffins from muffin cups. Serve warm. Makes 12 muffins.

Nutrition information per muffin: 172 calories, 2 g protein, 26 g carbohydrate, 7 g fat (1 g saturated), 18 mg cholesterol, 117 mg sodium.

Bacon Walnut Muffins

Bacon and thyme give a pleasant flavor blend to these savory muffins—great with salads or soups.

2¼ cups all-purpose flour
2 teaspoons baking powder
1 teaspoon snipped fresh thyme or
    ¼ teaspoon dried thyme, crushed
⅛ teaspoon salt
2 beaten eggs
1 cup milk
½ cup cooking oil
6 slices bacon, crisp-cooked, drained,
    and crumbled
½ cup chopped walnuts

Grease twelve 2½-inch muffin cups. Set aside. In a medium mixing bowl stir together the flour, baking powder, thyme, and salt. Make a well in the center of the flour mixture.

In another medium mixing bowl combine eggs, milk, and oil. Add all at once to flour mixture. Stir just till moistened (batter should be lumpy). Fold in crumbled bacon and walnuts.

Spoon batter into prepared muffin cups, filling each almost full. Bake in a 400° oven about 20 minutes or till golden brown. Cool in muffin cups on a wire rack for 5 minutes. Remove muffins from muffin cups. Serve warm. Makes 12 muffins.

Nutrition information per muffin: 232 calories, 6 g protein, 19 g carbohydrate, 15 g fat (3 g saturated), 40 mg cholesterol, 155 mg sodium.

Whole Kernel Corn Muffins

These cornmeal muffins have a Southwestern flair. The cornmeal gives them a slightly sweet flavor and a crumbly texture.

1 cup all-purpose flour
¾ cup cornmeal
3 tablespoons sugar
2 teaspoons baking powder
¼ teaspoon salt
1 beaten egg
¾ cup milk
¼ cup cooking oil
1 8¾-ounce can whole kernel corn, drained
2 tablespoons snipped fresh chives or finely chopped green onion

Grease twelve 4½-inch cactus-shaped corn stick pans or 2½-inch muffin cups. In a medium mixing bowl stir together the flour, cornmeal, sugar, baking powder, and salt. Make a well in the center of flour mixture.

In another medium mixing bowl combine egg, milk, and oil. Add all at once to flour mixture. Stir just till moistened (batter should be lumpy). Fold in corn and chives or green onion.

Spoon batter into prepared pans, filling each ⅔ full. Bake in a 400° oven for 18 to 20 minutes or till golden brown. Cool in pans on a wire rack for 5 minutes. Remove from pans. Serve warm. Makes 12 muffins.

Nutrition information per muffin: 144 calories, 3 g protein, 21 g carbohydrate, 6 g fat (1 g saturated), 19 mg cholesterol, 163 mg sodium.

Cottage Cheese Chive Biscuits

Cottage Cheese Chive Biscuits

These biscuits go well with any of your favorite comfort foods, such as homemade soups and stews.

- 2 cups all-purpose flour
- 2½ teaspoons baking powder
- ¼ teaspoon salt
- 6 tablespoons butter
- ¾ cup small-curd cottage cheese
- ⅔ cup milk
- 2 tablespoons snipped fresh chives or thinly sliced green onion tops

Line a baking sheet with foil; grease foil. In a medium mixing bowl stir together flour, baking powder, and salt. Using a pastry blender, cut in butter till mixture resembles coarse crumbs. Make a well in center of flour mixture. Add cottage cheese, milk, and chives or onion tops all at once. Stir just till moistened.

Drop dough by generous tablespoonfuls onto prepared baking sheet. Bake in a 425° oven for 15 to 18 minutes or till golden brown. Serve warm. Makes 12 biscuits.

Nutrition information per biscuit: 141 calories, 4 g protein, 16 g carbohydrate, 7 g fat (4 g saturated), 18 mg cholesterol, 238 mg sodium.

Berry Cornmeal Scones

Scones usually taste best when served warm and crusty with softened butter or cream cheese.

- 1¼ cups all-purpose flour
- ¾ cup cornmeal
- ¼ cup sugar
- 2 teaspoons baking powder
- ¼ teaspoon baking soda
- ¼ teaspoon salt
- ⅓ cup butter
- 1 teaspoon finely shredded lemon peel
- 1 cup fresh or frozen blueberries or raspberries, thawed
- ⅔ cup buttermilk
- 1 teaspoon vanilla

Stir together flour, cornmeal, sugar, baking powder, soda, and salt. Using a pastry blender, cut in butter till mixture resembles coarse crumbs. Add peel. Make a well in the center of mixture. Add berries, buttermilk, and vanilla all at once. Stir just till moistened.

Quickly knead dough on a lightly floured surface by folding and pressing gently for 10 to 12 strokes or till nearly smooth. Pat or lightly roll into an 8-inch circle on an ungreased baking sheet. Cut into 10 wedges, cutting only halfway through dough to score. Bake in a 400° oven for 20 to 25 minutes or till golden brown. Cut into wedges. Serve warm. Makes 10 scones.

Nutrition information per scone: 180 calories, 3 g protein, 27 g carbohydrate, 7 g fat (4 g saturated), 17 mg cholesterol, 238 mg sodium.

English Tea Scones

Tender and slightly sweet, these treats are perfect for breakfast or afternoon tea. Serve with softly whipped and sweetened whipping cream.

2½ cups all-purpose flour
  2 tablespoons sugar
  4 teaspoons baking powder
  ¼ teaspoon salt
  ⅓ cup butter, cut into pieces
  ¾ cup whipping cream
  2 beaten eggs
  ½ cup dried currants or snipped raisins
     Milk
     Sugar

In a medium mixing bowl stir together the flour, 2 tablespoons sugar, baking powder, and salt. Using a pastry blender, cut in butter till the mixture resembles coarse crumbs.

Make a well in the center of flour mixture. Add the whipping cream, eggs, and currants or raisins all at once. Using a fork, stir just till moistened.

Quickly knead dough on a lightly floured surface by folding and pressing gently for 10 to 12 strokes or till nearly smooth. Pat or lightly roll dough into an 8-inch square. Cut dough into sixteen 2-inch squares.

Place the scones about 1 inch apart on an ungreased baking sheet. Brush scones with milk and sprinkle with additional sugar.

Bake in a 400° oven for 12 to 14 minutes or till golden brown. Remove scones from baking sheet. Serve warm. Makes 16 scones.

Nutrition information per scone: 168 calories, 3 g protein, 20 g carbohydrate, 9 g fat (5 g saturated), 52 mg cholesterol, 176 mg sodium.

Sweet Potato Biscuits

Choose these thyme-scented biscuits for dinner or lunch. They're delightful with roast turkey, fried chicken, and glazed ham, as well as with pork roast and chops.

2   cups all-purpose flour
2   teaspoons baking powder
2   teaspoons snipped fresh thyme or
        ½ teaspoon dried thyme, crushed
½   teaspoon baking soda
½   teaspoon salt
¼   cup shortening
1   cup mashed cooked sweet potatoes
        or mashed canned sweet potatoes
½   cup milk
2   tablespoons brown sugar

In a medium mixing bowl stir together flour, baking powder, thyme, baking soda, and salt. Using a pastry blender, cut in shortening till the mixture resembles coarse crumbs. Make a well in center of flour mixture.

In another medium mixing bowl stir together sweet potatoes, milk, and brown sugar. Add all at once to flour mixture. Using a fork, stir just till moistened.

Quickly knead the dough on a lightly floured surface by folding and pressing gently for 10 to 12 strokes or till nearly smooth.

Pat or lightly roll dough to ½-inch thickness. Cut dough with a floured 2½-inch round cutter, dipping cutter into flour between cuts. Place about 1 inch apart on an ungreased baking sheet.

Bake in a 425° oven for 12 to 15 minutes or till golden brown. Remove biscuits from baking sheet. Serve warm. Makes 12 biscuits.

Nutrition information per biscuit: 149 calories, 3 g protein, 24 g carbohydrate, 5 g fat (1 g saturated), 1 mg cholesterol, 211 mg sodium.

Walnut Swirls

These lightly iced brown sugar-walnut rolls are fabulous with coffee or tea. They are a delectable quick-fix substitute for old-fashioned cinnamon yeast rolls.

1½ cups all-purpose flour
½ cup whole wheat flour
1 tablespoon baking powder
2 teaspoons granulated sugar
½ teaspoon cream of tartar
¼ teaspoon salt
½ cup shortening
⅔ cup milk
3 tablespoons butter or margarine,
　　softened
½ cup packed brown sugar
⅓ cup chopped walnuts
1 tablespoon all-purpose flour
½ cup sifted powdered sugar
2 to 3 teaspoons milk

Grease an 11x7x1½-inch or 9-inch round baking pan. Set aside. In a medium mixing bowl stir together the 1½ cups all-purpose flour, whole wheat flour, baking powder, granulated sugar, cream of tartar, and salt.

Using a pastry blender, cut in shortening till mixture resembles coarse crumbs. Make a well in center of flour mixture. Add ⅔ cup milk all at once. Using a fork, stir just till moistened.

Quickly knead dough on a lightly floured surface by folding and pressing gently for 10 to 12 strokes or till nearly smooth. Lightly roll dough into a 12x8-inch rectangle. Spread with butter or margarine.

In a small mixing bowl stir together the brown sugar, walnuts, and 1 tablespoon all-purpose flour. Sprinkle dough with brown sugar mixture. Starting from a long side, roll up jelly-roll style. Cut into 12 slices. Arrange slices, cut sides up, in the prepared pan. Bake in a 400° oven for 20 to 25 minutes or till golden brown.

Meanwhile, for icing, in a small mixing bowl combine powdered sugar and enough of the 2 to 3 teaspoons milk to make an icing of drizzling consistency. Remove rolls from baking pan and place on a wire rack. Drizzle with icing. Serve warm. Makes 12 rolls.

Nutrition information per roll: 248 calories, 3 g protein, 29 g carbohydrate, 14 g fat (4 g saturated), 9 mg cholesterol, 175 mg sodium.

Apple Allspice Bread

Like the other tea breads in this section, you'll find this bread slices best after 24 hours. Wrap the loaf in plastic wrap or foil before storing.

  2   cups all-purpose flour
  1   cup packed brown sugar
1½   teaspoons baking powder
  ¾   teaspoon ground allspice
  ½   teaspoon baking soda
  ¼   teaspoon salt
  ½   cup butter
  2   eggs
  ¼   cup milk
  1   large Granny Smith or other
        cooking apple, peeled, cored, and
        coarsely shredded (1 cup)
  ½   cup raisins or snipped pitted dates

Grease bottom and ½ inch up sides of a 9x5x3-inch loaf pan. Set aside.

In a large mixing bowl stir together flour, brown sugar, baking powder, allspice, baking soda, and salt. Using a pastry blender, cut in butter till mixture resembles coarse crumbs. Make a well in center of flour mixture.

In a medium mixing bowl beat together eggs and milk. Add shredded apple. Add egg mixture all at once to flour mixture. Stir just till moistened (batter should be lumpy). Fold in raisins or dates.

Pour the batter into the prepared loaf pan. Bake in a 350° oven for 60 to 65 minutes or till a wooden toothpick inserted near the center comes out clean. (If necessary, cover loosely with foil the last 10 to 15 minutes to prevent overbrowning.)

Cool in pan on a wire rack for 10 minutes. Remove from pan. Cool completely on rack. Wrap and store overnight before slicing. Makes 1 loaf (16 servings).

Nutrition information per serving: 175 calories, 3 g protein, 27 g carbohydrate, 7 g fat (4 g saturated), 42 mg cholesterol, 179 mg sodium.

Carrot-Zucchini Loaves

The carrots and zucchini add a confettilike look to these moist loaves. Perfect served plain, or spread slices with a thin layer of whipped cream cheese.

2½ cups all-purpose flour
½ cup toasted wheat germ
2 teaspoons baking powder
½ teaspoon baking soda
½ teaspoon salt
3 beaten eggs
1 cup granulated sugar
1 cup finely shredded zucchini
1 cup finely shredded carrot
½ cup packed brown sugar
½ cup cooking oil

Grease bottom and ½ inch up sides of two 8x4x2-inch loaf pans. Set aside.

In a large mixing bowl stir together flour, wheat germ, baking powder, baking soda, and salt. Make a well in the center of flour mixture.

In a medium mixing bowl combine eggs, granulated sugar, zucchini, carrot, brown sugar, and oil. Add all at once to flour mixture. Stir just till moistened (batter should be lumpy).

Pour the batter into the prepared loaf pans. Bake in a 350° oven for 45 to 55 minutes or till a wooden toothpick inserted near the centers comes out clean. (If necessary, cover loosely with foil the last 10 to 15 minutes to prevent overbrowning.)

Cool in pans on wire racks for 10 minutes. Remove from pans. Cool completely on racks. Wrap and store overnight before slicing. Makes 2 loaves (24 servings).

Nutrition information per serving: 151 calories, 3 g protein, 23 g carbohydrate, 6 g fat (1 g saturated), 27 mg cholesterol, 112 mg sodium.

Lemon Bread

Toasting the nuts for this tangy lemon bread intensifies their flavor. If you make two small loaves, you can freeze one for later.

½ cup butter
1 cup sugar
2 eggs
1⅔ cups all-purpose flour
¾ cup buttermilk
1½ teaspoons finely shredded lemon peel
½ teaspoon baking soda
¼ teaspoon salt
⅓ cup chopped almonds, walnuts, or pecans, toasted
Lemon Glaze
Lemon peel curls (optional)

Grease bottom and ½ inch up sides of an 8x4x2-inch loaf pan or two 7½x3½x2-inch loaf pans. Set aside.

In a large mixing bowl beat butter with an electric mixer on medium to high speed for 30 seconds. Add the sugar and beat about 5 minutes or till light and fluffy. Add eggs, one at a time, beating well after each. Add flour, buttermilk, shredded lemon peel, baking soda, and salt. Beat just till combined. Stir in nuts.

Pour batter into the prepared pan. Bake in a 350° oven about 45 minutes for 8-inch loaf (about 40 minutes for 7½-inch loaves) or till a wooden toothpick inserted near the center comes out clean. (If necessary, cover the loaf loosely with foil the last 10 to 15 minutes to prevent overbrowning.)

Cool in pan on a wire rack for 10 minutes. Remove from pan. Place on wire rack set over waxed paper.

Spoon Lemon Glaze over top. Cool completely on wire rack. Wrap and store overnight before slicing. If desired, garnish with lemon peel curls. Makes 1 large loaf or 2 small loaves (16 servings).

Lemon Glaze: In a small mixing bowl stir together 3 tablespoons *lemon juice* and 1 tablespoon *sugar* till sugar is dissolved.

Nutrition information per serving: 174 calories, 3 g protein, 24 g carbohydrate, 8 g fat (4 g saturated), 42 mg cholesterol, 151 mg sodium.

Crunchy Parmesan Corn Bread

Flecks of dried tomatoes and green onions give this herb-seasoned bread both color and flavor. Serve warm with soup or salad.

1 cup boiling water
¼ cup bulgur
   Yellow cornmeal
1 cup all-purpose flour
1 cup yellow cornmeal
⅓ cup grated Parmesan cheese
2 tablespoons sugar
1 tablespoon baking powder
½ teaspoon fennel seed
½ teaspoon dried basil, crushed
2 beaten eggs
1 cup milk
¼ cup olive oil or cooking oil
⅓ cup oil-packed dried tomatoes,
   drained and chopped, or diced
   pimiento, drained
⅓ cup sliced green onions

In a small mixing bowl pour boiling water over bulgur and let stand for 5 minutes. Drain. Meanwhile, grease the bottom and ½ inch up sides of a 6-cup soufflé dish, an 8x4x2-inch loaf pan, or a 9x5x3-inch loaf pan. Sprinkle the bottom and side with a little cornmeal. Set aside.

In a large mixing bowl stir together the flour, 1 cup cornmeal, Parmesan cheese, sugar, baking powder, fennel seed, and basil. Make a well in the center of the flour mixture.

In a medium mixing bowl combine eggs, milk, and oil. Stir in bulgur. Add egg mixture all at once to flour mixture. Stir just till moistened (batter should be lumpy). Fold in the dried tomatoes or pimiento and sliced green onions.

Pour batter into prepared dish. Bake in a 375° oven for 50 to 55 minutes or till a wooden toothpick inserted near the center comes out clean. (If necessary, cover loosely with foil the last 10 to 15 minutes to prevent overbrowning.)

Remove from the dish. Cool on a wire rack for 30 minutes. Serve warm. Makes 1 loaf (8 servings).

Nutrition information per serving: 269 calories, 8 g protein, 35 g carbohydrate, 11 g fat (3 g saturated), 59 mg cholesterol, 259 mg sodium.

Peanut Butter & Jelly Coffee Cake

Perfect for a quick breakfast treat with a glass of milk—especially on a cold wintry morning.

2 cups all-purpose flour
¾ cup packed brown sugar
2 teaspoons baking powder
¼ teaspoon baking soda
¼ teaspoon salt
1 cup milk
½ cup peanut butter
2 eggs
¼ cup butter, softened
1 cup strawberry or grape jelly
Crumb Topping

Grease a 13x9x2-inch baking pan. Set aside. In a large mixing bowl stir together flour, brown sugar, baking powder, baking soda, and salt. Add the milk, peanut butter, eggs, and butter. Beat with an electric mixer on low speed till combined. Beat on medium speed for 1 minute, scraping the side of the bowl constantly.

Spread about two-thirds of the batter into prepared baking pan. Stir jelly and spoon over batter. Drop remaining batter in small mounds on top of the jelly. Sprinkle with Crumb Topping. Bake in a 350° oven for 30 to 35 minutes or till golden brown. Serve warm. Makes 1 coffee cake (12 servings).

Crumb Topping: In a small mixing bowl stir together ½ cup packed *brown sugar* and ½ cup *all-purpose flour*. Cut in ¼ cup *peanut butter* and 3 tablespoons *butter* till mixture resembles coarse crumbs.

Nutrition information per serving: 400 calories, 8 g protein, 58 g carbohydrate, 16 g fat (6 g saturated), 55 mg cholesterol, 306 mg sodium.

Cinnamon Swirl Bread

The aroma of cinnamon bread is enough to wake even the sleepiest of sleepyheads. Discover the delights of this comfort food for breakfast, or anytime you're in need of some T.L.C. (Also pictured on the cover.)

4¾ to 5¼ cups all-purpose flour
1 package active dry yeast
1¼ cups milk
¼ cup granulated sugar
¼ cup butter
¾ teaspoon salt
2 eggs
½ cup chopped walnuts or pecans,
   toasted
½ cup packed brown sugar
2 teaspoons ground cinnamon
2 tablespoons butter, softened
   Sifted powdered sugar

In a large mixing bowl stir together 2 cups of the flour and the yeast. Heat and stir milk, ¼ cup sugar, ¼ cup butter, and salt just till warm (120° to 130°) and butter almost melts. Add to flour mixture. Add eggs. Beat with an electric mixer on low to medium speed for 30 seconds, scraping bowl. Beat on high speed for 3 minutes. Stir in as much remaining flour as you can.

On a lightly floured surface, knead in enough of the remaining flour to make a moderately stiff dough that is smooth and elastic (6 to 8 minutes total). Shape into a ball. Place in a lightly greased bowl, turning once to grease surface. Cover and let rise in a warm place till double in size (about 1 hour). Punch down. Turn dough out onto lightly floured surface. Divide in half. Cover and let rest for 10 minutes.

Meanwhile, grease two 9x5x3-inch or 8x4x2-inch loaf pans. Set aside. For filling, in a small bowl stir together the nuts, brown sugar, and cinnamon. Roll each portion of dough into a 14x8-inch rectangle. Spread each with 1 tablespoon butter and sprinkle with half of the filling. For each loaf, starting from both short sides, roll up each side jelly-roll style toward center. Place, rolled sides up, in the prepared loaf pans. Cover and let rise till nearly double (about 30 minutes).

Bake in a 350° oven for 30 to 35 minutes or till bread sounds hollow when lightly tapped. (If necessary, cover loosely with foil the last 10 minutes to prevent overbrowning.) Remove from pans. Cool. Sprinkle with powdered sugar. Makes 2 loaves (32 servings).

Nutrition information per serving: 123 calories, 3 g protein, 19 g carbohydrate, 4 g fat (2 g saturated), 20 mg cholesterol, 82 mg sodium.

Almond-Filled Hearts

Offer these pretty hearts as an afternoon treat with a cup of coffee or as a breakfast roll on special occasions.

4   to 4⅓ cups all-purpose flour
1   package active dry yeast
1   cup milk
¼   cup butter
3   tablespoons granulated sugar
½   teaspoon salt
2   eggs
     Almond Filling
     Milk
     Coarse sugar (optional)

In a large bowl stir together 2 cups of the flour and yeast. Heat and stir 1 cup milk, butter, 3 tablespoons sugar, and salt just till warm (120° to 130°) and butter almost melts. Add to flour mixture. Add eggs. Beat with an electric mixer on low to medium speed for 30 seconds, scraping bowl. Beat on high speed for 3 minutes. Stir in as much of the remaining flour as you can. On a lightly floured surface, knead in enough remaining flour to make a moderately soft dough that is smooth and elastic (3 to 5 minutes total). Shape into a ball. Place in a lightly greased bowl, turning once. Cover and let rise in a warm place till double in size (about 1 hour). Punch down. Turn out onto lightly floured surface. Cover and let rest for 10 minutes.

Meanwhile, grease 2 large baking sheets. Set aside. Roll dough into a 27x10-inch rectangle. Cut into twelve 10x2¼-inch strips. Divide the Almond Filling into 12 portions. Roll each into a 9½-inch-long rope. Place a rope lengthwise down center of each strip of dough. Fold dough in half lengthwise to enclose filling. Moisten edges of dough; pinch well to seal. Place, seam sides down, on prepared baking sheets. Form each filled strip into a heart shape. Moisten ends and pinch together at base of heart to seal.

Cover and let rise in a warm place till nearly double (30 to 40 minutes). If desired, brush with a little milk and sprinkle with coarse sugar. Bake in a 350° oven for 12 to 15 minutes or till golden brown. Remove from baking sheets. Cool on wire racks. Makes 12 hearts.

Almond Filling: Beat together one 8-ounce can *almond paste*, crumbled; ¼ cup *granulated sugar*; 1 *egg yolk*; and 1 tablespoon *all-purpose flour.*

Nutrition information per heart: 318 calories, 9 g protein, 47 g carbohydrate, 11 g fat (4 g saturated), 65 mg cholesterol, 152 mg sodium.

Overnight Bubble Loaf

This yeast loaf is a great choice for a make-ahead bread. It waits in the refrigerator, shaped and ready to bake.

3½ to 4 cups all-purpose flour
1 package active dry yeast
1⅓ cups milk
2 tablespoons honey
1 tablespoon butter
¾ teaspoon salt
1 egg
⅔ cup toasted wheat germ
⅔ cup packed brown sugar
¼ cup butter
3 tablespoons light-colored corn syrup
½ teaspoon ground cinnamon
⅓ cup chopped walnuts
⅓ cup granulated sugar
1 teaspoon ground cinnamon
3 tablespoons butter, melted

In a large mixing bowl stir together 1½ cups of the flour and the yeast. In a medium saucepan heat and stir milk, honey, 1 tablespoon butter, and salt just till warm (120° to 130°) and butter almost melts. Add to flour mixture. Add egg. Beat with an electric mixer on low to medium speed for 30 seconds, scraping bowl. Beat on high speed for 3 minutes. Stir in wheat germ and as much of the remaining flour as you can.

On a lightly floured surface, knead in enough of the remaining flour to make a moderately soft dough that is smooth and elastic (3 to 5 minutes total). Shape into a ball. Place in a lightly greased bowl, turning once to grease surface. Cover and let rest for 20 minutes. Meanwhile, grease a 10-inch fluted tube pan. In a saucepan heat and stir brown sugar, ¼ cup butter, corn syrup, and ½ teaspoon cinnamon till butter is melted.

Divide dough into 16 pieces. Roll each piece into a ball. Place walnuts in bottom of prepared pan. Combine ⅓ cup sugar and 1 teaspoon cinnamon. Dip balls of dough in the melted butter and coat with cinnamon mixture. Place half of the coated balls in a single layer in prepared pan. Drizzle with about one-third of the brown sugar mixture. Top with remaining coated balls and drizzle with remaining brown sugar mixture. Cover lightly with oiled waxed paper, then plastic wrap, and chill for 2 to 24 hours.

Uncover and let stand about 20 minutes. Bake in a 350° oven for 35 to 40 minutes or till bread sounds hollow when lightly tapped. Cool in pan on a wire rack for 5 minutes. Turn bread out onto a platter. Cool for 45 minutes. Makes 1 loaf (16 servings).

Nutrition information per serving: 256 calories, 6 g protein, 40 g carbohydrate, 9 g fat (4 g saturated), 30 mg cholesterol, 178 mg sodium.

Cheddar Batter Bread

Batter breads are a quick way to a homemade loaf of yeast bread. There is no kneading and they require just one rising time. Mix and let rise in the baking pan.

1   tablespoon cornmeal
2   cups all-purpose flour
1   package active dry yeast
¼   teaspoon onion powder
¼   teaspoon black pepper
1   cup milk
2   tablespoons sugar
2   tablespoons butter
¼   teaspoon salt
1   egg
¾   cup shredded cheddar or Monterey
      Jack cheese with jalapeño peppers
      (3 ounces)
½   cup cornmeal

Grease an 8x4x2-inch loaf pan and sprinkle with the 1 tablespoon cornmeal. Set aside.

In a large mixing bowl stir together 1½ cups of the flour, the yeast, onion powder, and black pepper. In a small saucepan heat and stir milk, sugar, butter, and salt just till warm (120° to 130°) and butter almost melts. Add to flour mixture. Add egg.

Beat with an electric mixer on low to medium speed for 30 seconds, scraping the side of bowl constantly. Beat on high speed for 3 minutes. Using a wooden spoon, stir in cheese, ½ cup cornmeal, and remaining flour (batter should be soft and sticky).

Turn the batter into the prepared pan. Cover and let rise in a warm place till nearly double (about 1 hour).

Bake in a 350° oven about 40 minutes or till bread sounds hollow when lightly tapped. (If necessary, cover loosely with foil the last 15 minutes to prevent overbrowning.)

Immediately remove bread from pan. Cool on a wire rack. Makes 1 loaf (16 servings).

Nutrition information per serving: 124 calories, 4 g protein, 17 g carbohydrate, 4 g fat (2 g saturated), 24 mg cholesterol, 93 mg sodium.

Onion Mustard Sandwich Buns

For frankfurter buns, shape squares of dough into 4- to 5-inch-long rolls, tapering ends. Place on greased baking sheets and flatten each with the palm of your hand. Bake as for round-shaped buns.

5¼ to 5¾ cups all-purpose flour
1 package active dry yeast
2 cups milk
2 tablespoons sugar
2 tablespoons dried minced onion
2 tablespoons cooking oil
2 tablespoons prepared mustard
1 teaspoon salt
½ teaspoon freshly ground pepper
2 eggs
2 tablespoons water
4 teaspoons dried minced onion
 Poppy seed

In a large mixing bowl stir together 2 cups of the flour and the yeast. Heat and stir milk, sugar, 2 tablespoons onion, oil, mustard, salt, and pepper just till warm (120° to 130°). Add to flour mixture. Add 1 egg. Beat with an electric mixer on low to medium speed for 30 seconds, scraping bowl. Beat on high speed for 3 minutes. Stir in as much remaining flour as you can.

On a lightly floured surface, knead in enough of the remaining flour to make a moderately soft dough that is smooth and elastic (3 to 5 minutes total). Shape into a ball. Place in a lightly greased bowl, turning once to grease surface. Cover and let rise in a warm place till double in size (about 1 hour).

Punch down. Turn dough out onto lightly floured surface. Divide in half. Cover and let rest for 10 minutes. Meanwhile, grease 2 large baking sheets.

Pat each portion of dough into a 9-inch square. Cut each into nine 3-inch squares. Tuck corners under to form balls. Place on the prepared baking sheets. Flatten with the palm of your hand. Cover and let rise till nearly double (30 to 40 minutes).

In a small bowl combine 1 egg and water. Brush buns with some of the egg mixture. Bake in a 350° oven for 20 minutes. Brush buns again with egg mixture and sprinkle with 4 teaspoons onion and a little poppy seed. Bake about 5 minutes more or till buns are golden brown and onion is toasted. Remove from baking sheets. Cool on wire racks. Makes 18 buns.

Nutrition information per bun: 169 calories, 5 g protein, 29 g carbohydrate, 3 g fat (1 g saturated), 26 mg cholesterol, 162 mg sodium.

Cloverleaf Rye Rolls

To make these rolls ahead, wrap the cooled, baked rolls in a single layer of heavy foil. Seal, label, and freeze up to 2 months. To reheat, place wrapped frozen rolls in a 350° oven for 30 to 35 minutes.

3½ to 4 cups all-purpose flour
2 packages active dry yeast
2 cups water
¼ cup sugar
2 tablespoons shortening
1 teaspoon salt
2 cups rye flour
Butter or margarine, melted
(optional)

In a large mixing bowl stir together 2¾ cups of the all-purpose flour and the yeast. In a medium saucepan heat and stir water, sugar, shortening, and salt just till warm (120° to 130°) and shortening almost melts. Add to flour mixture. Beat with an electric mixer on low to medium speed for 30 seconds, scraping bowl constantly. Beat on high speed for 3 minutes. Using a wooden spoon, stir in rye flour and as much of the remaining all-purpose flour as you can.

On a lightly floured surface, knead in enough of the remaining all-purpose flour to make a moderately soft dough that is smooth and elastic (3 to 5 minutes total). Shape into a ball. Place in a lightly greased bowl, turning once to grease surface. Cover and let rise in a warm place till double in size (about 1 hour).

Punch dough down. Turn dough out onto lightly floured surface. Divide in half. Cover and let rest for 10 minutes. Meanwhile, lightly grease twenty-four 2½-inch muffin cups.

Divide each portion of dough into 36 pieces. Shape each piece into a ball, pulling edges under to make a smooth top. Place 3 balls in each muffin cup, smooth sides up. Cover and let rise in a warm place till nearly double (about 30 minutes).

Bake in a 375° oven for 15 to 18 minutes or till golden brown. If desired, brush with melted butter or margarine. Remove from muffin cups. Cool on wire racks or serve warm. Makes 24 rolls.

Nutrition information per roll: 110 calories, 3 g protein, 22 g carbohydrate, 1 g fat (0 g saturated), 0 mg cholesterol, 90 mg sodium.

Mixed Berry Pie

Showcase the summer's best berries in this cream-of-the-crop pie.

Pastry for Double-Crust Pie
1 cup sugar
3 tablespoons cornstarch
1 teaspoon finely shredded orange
    peel
½ teaspoon ground cinnamon
¼ teaspoon ground nutmeg
⅛ teaspoon ground ginger
2 cups sliced strawberries
2 cups blackberries or raspberries
1 cup blueberries
    Milk
    Sugar

Prepare Pastry for Double-Crust Pie. On a lightly floured surface, roll out half of the pastry. Ease into a 9-inch pie plate. Set aside.

For filling, in a large mixing bowl combine 1 cup sugar, cornstarch, orange peel, cinnamon, nutmeg, and ginger. Add strawberries, blackberries or raspberries, and blueberries. Toss gently to coat.

Transfer the filling to the pastry-lined pie plate. Trim pastry even with edge of pie plate. Roll out remaining pastry; cut slits in pastry. Place on top of filling. Seal and flute edge. Cover edge with foil. Brush pastry with a little milk and sprinkle with additional sugar.

Bake in a 375° oven for 25 minutes. Remove foil. Bake for 20 to 25 minutes more or till crust is golden brown and filling is bubbly. Cool slightly on a wire rack. Serve warm. Makes 8 servings.

Pastry for Double-Crust Pie: In a large bowl stir together 2 cups *all-purpose flour* and ½ teaspoon *salt*. Using a pastry blender, cut in ⅔ cup *shortening* till pieces are pea-size. Using 6 to 7 tablespoons *cold water,* sprinkle 1 tablespoon water at a time over mixture, gently tossing with a fork till all is moistened. Divide in half. Form each half into a ball.

Nutrition information per serving: 411 calories, 4 g protein, 61 g carbohydrate, 18 g fat (4 g saturated), 0 mg cholesterol, 137 mg sodium.

Cherry-Pear Pie

The surprise ingredient in this pie is a subtle hint of rosemary that enhances the fresh fruit flavors of the ripe pears and red cherries.

⅔ cup granulated sugar
3 tablespoons cornstarch
¼ teaspoon ground nutmeg
¼ teaspoon dried rosemary, crushed (optional)
4 cups thinly sliced, peeled pears
3 cups frozen pitted tart red cherries
   Pastry for Double-Crust Pie (see recipe, opposite)
1 beaten egg white
1 tablespoon water
   Coarse sugar
   Vanilla ice cream (optional)

For filling, in a large mixing bowl stir together ⅔ cup sugar, cornstarch, nutmeg, and, if desired, rosemary. Add pears and frozen cherries. Toss gently to coat. Let stand at room temperature for 20 minutes.

Meanwhile, prepare Pastry for Double-Crust Pie. On a lightly floured surface, roll out half of the pastry. Ease into a 9-inch pie plate.

Transfer the filling to the pastry-lined pie plate. Trim pastry even with edge of pie plate. Roll out remaining pastry. Using a miniature heart cookie cutter, cut out shapes from center of pastry. Set cutouts aside. Place the pastry on top of filling. Seal and flute edge. Cover the edge with foil.

In a small bowl combine egg white and water. Brush pastry with some of the egg white mixture. Top with pastry cutouts. Brush again with egg white mixture. Sprinkle with coarse sugar.

Bake in a 375° oven for 25 minutes. Remove foil. Bake for 30 to 35 minutes more or till crust is golden brown. Cool slightly on a wire rack. Serve warm. If desired, serve with ice cream. Makes 8 servings.

Nutrition information per serving: 418 calories, 4 g protein, 62 g carbohydrate, 18 g fat (4 g saturated), 0 mg cholesterol, 143 mg sodium.

No-Peel Apple Pie

The expression "easy-as-pie" surely applies to this treat. Pick a thin-skinned apple, such as Golden Delicious, Jonagold, or Jonathan, to make it.

1 15-ounce package (2 crusts) folded
    refrigerated unbaked piecrust
6 large cooking apples
½ cup water
2 tablespoons lemon juice
½ cup granulated sugar
2 tablespoons all-purpose flour
1½ teaspoons apple pie spice
    Whipping cream or milk
    Coarse and/or granulated sugar

Let piecrust stand at room temperature according to package directions. Unfold piecrust. Ease one crust into a 9-inch pie plate. Set aside.

For filling, core and slice unpeeled apples (you should have 8 cups). In a large bowl combine the apples, water, and lemon juice. Toss gently to coat. In another large bowl stir together the ½ cup sugar, flour, and apple pie spice. Drain the apples well; add to sugar mixture. Toss gently to coat.

Transfer the filling to the pastry-lined pie plate. Trim pastry even with edge of pie plate. Cut out desired small shapes from center of the remaining piecrust; set cutouts aside.

Place piecrust on top of filling. Seal and flute edge. Cover edge with foil. Brush the pastry with a little whipping cream or milk. Top with pastry cutouts. Brush again with cream or milk. Sprinkle with coarse and/or granulated sugar.

Bake in a 375° oven for 30 minutes. Remove foil. Bake about 30 minutes more or till crust is golden. Cool slightly on a wire rack. Serve warm. Makes 8 servings.

Nutrition information per serving: 373 calories, 2 g protein, 58 g carbohydrate, 16 g fat (1 g saturated), 18 mg cholesterol, 211 mg sodium.

Eggnog Custard Pie

Ring in the holidays with this smooth, spiced pie made with a time-honored yuletide treat.

Pastry for Single-Crust Pie
4 eggs
2¼ cups dairy or canned eggnog
½ cup sugar
2 tablespoons light rum
1 teaspoon vanilla
¼ teaspoon salt
Ground nutmeg

Prepare Pastry for Single-Crust Pie. On a lightly floured surface, roll out the pastry. Ease pastry into a 9-inch pie plate. Trim the pastry even with edge of pie plate. Flute edge.

Line pastry with a double thickness of foil. Bake in a 450° oven for 8 minutes. Remove foil. Bake for 4 to 5 minutes more or till pastry is set and dry. Reduce the oven temperature to 350°.

Meanwhile, for filling, in a large mixing bowl beat eggs slightly with a rotary beater or fork. Stir in eggnog, sugar, rum, vanilla, and salt.

Place the partially baked pastry shell on the oven rack. Carefully pour the filling into the pastry shell. Sprinkle with nutmeg. Cover edge of pie with foil.

Bake in the 350° oven for 25 minutes. Remove foil. Bake for 15 to 20 minutes more or till a knife inserted near the center comes out clean. Cool on a wire rack for 1 to 2 hours. Refrigerate within 2 hours; cover for longer storage. Makes 8 servings.

Pastry for Single-Crust Pie: In a medium bowl stir together 1¼ cups *all-purpose flour* and ¼ teaspoon *salt*. Using a pastry blender, cut in ⅓ cup *shortening* till pieces are pea-size. Using 4 to 5 tablespoons *cold water*, sprinkle 1 tablespoon water at a time over mixture, gently tossing with a fork till all is moistened. Form dough into a ball.

Nutrition information per serving: 327 calories, 7 g protein, 36 g carbohydrate, 16 g fat (3 g saturated), 107 mg cholesterol, 210 mg sodium.

Pumpkin-Cream Cheese Pie

This special pie—with its rich creamy base, spicy pumpkin layer, and nutty topping—catapults the Thanksgiving standard into pumpkin-pie paradise.

Pastry for Single-Crust Pie (see recipe, opposite)
1   8-ounce package cream cheese, softened
½   cup granulated sugar
3   eggs
½   teaspoon vanilla
1¼ cups canned pumpkin
1   cup evaporated milk
¼   cup packed brown sugar
1   teaspoon ground cinnamon
¼   teaspoon salt
¼   teaspoon ground nutmeg
½   cup chopped pecans
2   tablespoons all-purpose flour
2   tablespoons brown sugar
1   tablespoon butter, softened
    Whipped cream (optional)
    Ground nutmeg (optional)

Prepare Pastry for Single-Crust Pie. On a lightly floured surface, roll out the pastry. Ease into a 9-inch pie plate. Trim the pastry even with edge of pie plate. Flute edge. Set aside.

In a small mixing bowl beat together the cream cheese, ¼ cup of the granulated sugar, 1 of the eggs, and vanilla with an electric mixer on low to medium speed till smooth. Cover and chill for 30 minutes. Spoon into pastry-lined pie plate.

In a medium bowl combine the pumpkin, evaporated milk, remaining granulated sugar, remaining eggs, ¼ cup brown sugar, cinnamon, salt, and ¼ teaspoon nutmeg. Carefully pour over cream cheese mixture.

Cover edge of pie with foil. Bake in a 350° oven for 25 minutes. Remove foil. Bake for 25 minutes more.

Meanwhile, in a small bowl combine pecans, flour, 2 tablespoons brown sugar, and butter. Sprinkle over the pie. Bake for 10 to 15 minutes more or till a knife inserted near the center comes out clean.

Cool pie on a wire rack for 1 to 2 hours. Refrigerate within 2 hours; cover for longer storage. If desired, top each serving with whipped cream and additional nutmeg. Makes 8 servings.

Nutrition information per serving: 477 calories, 10 g protein, 46 g carbohydrate, 29 g fat (11 g saturated), 122 mg cholesterol, 295 mg sodium.

Banana Split Cake

Looking for a star dessert for your next gathering? This one wins rave reviews for its soda fountain flavors.

1 package 2-layer-size banana
   cake mix
   Sweetened Whipped Cream or
   6 ounces frozen whipped dessert
   topping, thawed
1 cup sliced strawberries
1 8¼-ounce can crushed pineapple,
   well drained
1 11- to 12-ounce jar fudge ice-cream
   topping
½ cup coarsely chopped peanuts
   Banana slices (optional)

Prepare the banana cake mix according to package directions for a two-layer cake. Cool completely.

For fillings, divide the Sweetened Whipped Cream or dessert topping in half. Fold strawberries into half of the whipped cream. Fold drained pineapple into the remaining whipped cream. In a small saucepan heat and stir fudge ice-cream topping over low heat just till warm (not hot).

To assemble, using a serrated knife, split each cake layer in half horizontally. Place bottom of 1 split layer on serving plate. Top with the strawberry filling, spreading to edge of layer. Top with another split layer. Spread with half of the fudge topping, letting some drizzle down side. Sprinkle with half of the nuts.

Top with another split layer. Spread with pineapple filling. Top with remaining split layer. Spread with remaining fudge topping, letting some drizzle down side of cake. Sprinkle with the remaining nuts.

Serve immediately. (Or, cover loosely with plastic wrap, placing a few toothpicks in top of cake so wrap doesn't stick to topping, and chill up to 2 hours.) If desired, garnish with banana slices. Makes 12 servings.

Sweetened Whipped Cream: In a chilled medium bowl combine 1 cup *whipping cream*, 2 tablespoons *sugar*, and ½ teaspoon *vanilla*. Beat with an electric mixer on medium to high speed till soft peaks form (tips curl).

Nutrition information per serving: 494 calories, 7 g protein, 67 g carbohydrate, 24 g fat (10 g saturated), 63 mg cholesterol, 222 mg sodium.

Pumpkin-Pear Cake

No frosting needed! When you invert this upside-down-style cake, a smooth, caramel syrup oozes over the pears and warm pumpkin cake.

⅓ cup packed brown sugar
2 tablespoons butter, melted
1 tablespoon water
2 medium pears, peeled and sliced
1¼ cups all-purpose flour
1¼ teaspoons baking powder
1 teaspoon pumpkin pie spice
¼ teaspoon baking soda
3 egg whites
¾ cup granulated sugar
¾ cup canned pumpkin
⅓ cup cooking oil
2 tablespoons water
1 teaspoon vanilla
  Orange peel curls (optional)

In a small bowl combine the brown sugar, melted butter, and 1 tablespoon water. Pour into an ungreased 9x1½-inch round baking pan. Arrange the pear slices in pan. Set aside.

In a small mixing bowl combine flour, baking powder, pumpkin pie spice, and baking soda. Set aside. In another small mixing bowl beat egg whites with an electric mixer on medium to high speed till soft peaks form (tips curl). Gradually add the granulated sugar, beating till stiff peaks form (tips stand straight).

Add pumpkin, oil, 2 tablespoons water, and vanilla, beating on low speed till combined. Fold in the flour mixture just till moistened. Carefully spoon over pears. Spread mixture evenly with the back of a spoon.

Bake in a 350° oven about 35 minutes or till a wooden toothpick inserted near the center comes out clean. Cool in pan on a wire rack for 5 minutes. Invert onto a serving plate. Serve warm. If desired, garnish with orange peel curls. Makes 10 servings.

Nutrition information per serving: 250 calories, 3 g protein, 39 g carbohydrate, 10 g fat (3 g saturated), 6 mg cholesterol, 120 mg sodium.

Buttermilk-Pineapple Carrot Cake

A decadent version of the classic, this cake adds pineapple, coconut, and a luscious buttermilk glaze layer.
Consider the 13x9-inch size when toting.

2	cups all-purpose flour
2	cups granulated sugar
2	teaspoons baking soda
1½	teaspoons ground cinnamon
1	teaspoon baking powder
¼	teaspoon salt
2	cups finely shredded carrots*
1	8¼-ounce can crushed pineapple, drained
1	cup chopped walnuts
3	eggs
½	cup coconut
¼	cup buttermilk or sour milk
¼	cup cooking oil
1	teaspoon vanilla
	Buttermilk Glaze
	Cream Cheese Frosting
½	cup chopped walnuts

Grease a 13x9x2-inch baking pan or grease and lightly flour two 9x1½-inch round baking pans. Set aside.

In a large mixing bowl combine flour, granulated sugar, baking soda, cinnamon, baking powder, and salt. Add carrots, drained pineapple, 1 cup nuts, eggs, coconut, buttermilk or sour milk, oil, and vanilla. Stir till combined. Pour into the prepared pan.

Bake in a 350° oven for 40 to 45 minutes or till top springs back when lightly touched. Pour Buttermilk Glaze evenly over top of cake. Place 13x9-inch pan on a wire rack; cool completely. (Or, cool layer cakes in pans on wire racks for 15 minutes. Remove from pans. Cool completely on racks.) Frost with Cream Cheese Frosting. Sprinkle with ½ cup nuts. Cover and store in the refrigerator. Makes 16 servings.

Buttermilk Glaze: In a small saucepan bring ½ cup *granulated sugar*, ¼ cup *buttermilk* or *sour milk*, ¼ cup *butter*, and 2 teaspoons light-colored *corn syrup* to boiling; reduce heat. Cook and stir for 4 minutes. Remove from heat. Stir in ½ teaspoon *vanilla*.

Cream Cheese Frosting: Beat two 3-ounce packages softened *cream cheese*, ½ cup softened *butter*, and 2 teaspoons *vanilla* with an electric mixer till light and fluffy. Gradually beat in 2 cups sifted *powdered sugar*. Gradually beat in 2½ to 2¾ cups additional sifted *powdered sugar* to make of spreading consistency.

*Note: The carrots need to be finely shredded or they may sink to the bottom of the pan during baking.

Nutrition information per serving: 544 calories, 6 g protein, 79 g carbohydrate, 25 g fat (10 g saturated), 75 mg cholesterol, 360 mg sodium.

Jam Thumbprints

Have these cookies baked, cooled, and on hand for drop-in company. Fill them right before serving.

⅔ cup butter
½ cup sugar
2 egg yolks
1 teaspoon vanilla
1½ cups all-purpose flour
2 slightly beaten egg whites
1 cup finely chopped walnuts
⅓ to ½ cup apricot, strawberry, or cherry jam or preserves

Grease a cookie sheet. Set aside. In a large mixing bowl beat butter with an electric mixer on medium to high speed for 30 seconds. Add sugar; beat till combined, scraping side of bowl occasionally.

Beat in egg yolks and vanilla till combined. Beat in as much of the flour as you can with the mixer. Stir in the remaining flour. Cover and chill about 1 hour or till easy to handle.

Shape dough into 1-inch balls. Roll balls in egg whites, then coat with walnuts. Place about 1 inch apart on the prepared cookie sheet. Press your thumb into the center of each ball.

Bake in a 375° oven for 10 to 12 minutes or till edges are lightly browned. Transfer to a wire rack; cool. Before serving, fill centers of cookies with jam or preserves. Makes about 42 cookies.

Nutrition information per cookie: 79 calories, 1 g protein, 8 g carbohydrate, 5 g fat (2 g saturated), 18 mg cholesterol, 33 mg sodium.

Pecan Drops

Pick out the nicest pecan halves to use for the cookie tops and chop the rest to stir into the dough.

½ cup butter
2 cups sifted powdered sugar
1¾ cups all-purpose flour
⅓ cup milk
1 egg
1 teaspoon baking powder
1 teaspoon vanilla
1 cup coarsely chopped pecans
   Granulated sugar
   Pecan halves (optional)

Lightly grease a cookie sheet. Set aside. In a large mixing bowl beat butter with an electric mixer on medium to high speed for 30 seconds.

Add powdered sugar, about half of the flour, about half of the milk, the egg, baking powder, and vanilla. Beat till combined, scraping side of bowl occasionally. Beat or stir in the remaining flour and the remaining milk. Stir in the chopped pecans.

Drop dough by a rounded teaspoon about 2 inches apart onto the prepared cookie sheet. Sprinkle with granulated sugar. If desired, lightly press a pecan half in the center of each cookie.

Bake in a 375° oven for 8 to 10 minutes or till edges are lightly browned. Transfer to a wire rack; cool. Makes about 36 cookies.

Nutrition information per cookie: 90 calories, 1 g protein, 11 g carbohydrate, 5 g fat (1 g saturated), 9 mg cholesterol, 36 mg sodium.

Drop Cookie Hints

For attractive drop cookies, use a spoon from your flatware set—not a measuring spoon—to drop them, keeping the mounds the same size and spacing them evenly on the cookie sheet. Don't crowd the mounds. When a recipe calls for a greased cookie sheet, use only a light coating of shortening. A heavy coating will cause the cookies to spread too much. Also, don't drop the dough onto a hot cookie sheet. The heat will cause the cookies to flatten. Instead, use two sheets or cool one sheet between batches.

Easy Fudge Brownies

These no-mixing-bowl brownies are a breeze to make. Mix them in a saucepan, pour them into a baking pan, and enjoy them in no time.

½   cup butter
2   ounces unsweetened chocolate, chopped
1   cup sugar
2   eggs
1   teaspoon vanilla
¾   cup all-purpose flour
½   cup chopped nuts

Grease an 8x8x2-inch baking pan. Set aside. In a medium saucepan heat butter and chocolate till melted, stirring occasionally. Remove from heat. Stir in sugar, eggs, and vanilla. Using a wooden spoon, lightly beat mixture just till combined (don't overbeat or brownies will rise too high then fall). Stir in flour and chopped nuts. Spread batter in prepared pan.

Bake in a 350° oven for 30 minutes. Cool in pan on a wire rack. Cut into bars. Makes 24 brownies.

Nutrition information per brownie: 113 calories, 2 g protein, 12 g carbohydrate, 7 g fat (3 g saturated), 28 mg cholesterol, 44 mg sodium.

Brickle Bars: Prepare as above, except omit the nuts. Spread batter in prepared pan and sprinkle with ¾ cup *almond brickle pieces* and ½ cup *miniature semisweet chocolate pieces*. Bake. Cool in pan on a wire rack.

Brickle Bars

Saucepan Oatmeal Cookies

Dress up these super-simple cookies: Heat ½ cup semisweet chocolate pieces with 1 tablespoon shortening over low heat just till melted, stirring occasionally. Drizzle over cooled cookies.

1	cup granulated sugar
1	cup packed brown sugar
1	cup butter
3	cups quick-cooking rolled oats
1¼	cups all-purpose flour
1	teaspoon baking powder
1	teaspoon baking soda
¼	teaspoon salt
2	beaten eggs
½	cup coconut, chopped (optional)

Grease a cookie sheet. Set aside. In a medium saucepan combine granulated sugar, brown sugar, and butter. Cook and stir over medium heat till butter is melted. Remove from heat. Stir in oats, flour, baking powder, baking soda, and salt till combined. Add eggs; mix well. If desired, stir in coconut.

Drop batter by a rounded teaspoon about 3 inches apart onto the prepared cookie sheet, stirring batter often. Bake in a 375° oven for 6 to 7 minutes or till edges are firm. Cool on cookie sheet for 1 minute. Transfer to a wire rack; cool. Makes about 48 cookies.

Nutrition information per cookie: 102 calories, 1 g protein, 14 g carbohydrate, 5 g fat (1 g saturated), 14 mg cholesterol, 85 mg sodium.

Margarine in Baking

The recipes in this book call for butter, not margarine, because it ensures the best results. Although baked goods made with some margarines can be satisfactory, choosing the right margarine is tricky. Many margarines contain more water than oil, which will yield undesirable results. If you choose to use margarine, select a stick margarine that lists at least 80 percent vegetable oil or 100 calories per tablespoon on the package. Diet, whipped, liquid, and soft spreads or margarines are for table use— not baking. Their high water content can make baked goods wet and tough.

INDEX